# LET US PRAY

MARIA HERNANDEZ

To order additional copies of this book, contact:
Xlibris
844-714-8691
www.Xlibris.com
Orders@Xlibris.com

ISBN:    Softcover        978-1-6641-9926-2
         EBook            978-1-6641-9925-5

Print information available on the last page

Rev. date: 05/24/2022

# LETTER TO THE PARENTS

You will find this account of Daniel from the book of Daniel chapter 2. This account has been simplified to allow for understanding of the purpose of prayer. May the Lord greatly bless each and every one of you as you endeavor to train up your child in the way he/she should go. (Proverbs 22:6)

Love, in Christ,

Maria Hernandez

# LET US PRAY

What is prayer? How are we supposed to pray?
What happens when we pray?

In the Bible, one example of prayer is found in the book of Daniel. When Daniel was a teenager, he became a servant to the Babylonian king named Nebuchadnezzar.

One night, King Nebuchadnezzar dreamed. The dreams became so frightening they startled him awake. His mind, filled with fear, prevented him from being able to go back to sleep.

To make matters worse, he couldn't remember what he had dreamed! As frightened as he was, he just couldn't remember why the dreams had scared him. The king decided he would have all the magicians, sorcerers, and astrologers in his kingdom gathered together. Once they were in front of him, he demanded they tell him what he had dreamed and the meaning of his dreams.

Of course, no one could tell the king what he had dreamed! And if they didn't know what he had dreamed, there was no way they could reveal their meaning. They told the king no one could answer his question and his demand was unreasonable. No other king had ever made such a request.

The king became furious! He sent his soldiers to make sure all the magicians, sorcerers, and astrologers were gathered together to be punished.

When Daniel learned what was happening, he asked God for help. He spoke to God about the king's demands and the fear of punishment by the king. Daniel prayed by talking to God.

God responded by giving Daniel the same dreams and the ability to understand them. When Daniel told the king what God had revealed, King Nebuchadnezzar gave glory to God and proclaimed, "Surely your God is the God of gods and the Lord of kings." Prayer includes God responding to our prayers.

Prayer is communication with God. Daniel spoke to God about his concerns and of the occurrences happening. God responded to Daniel's prayers by answering Daniel's requests. In the end, Daniel was saved from the king's punishment.

Isn't it wonderful to know God hears our prayers?

Why don't we pray together right now?

## PRAYER

Dear Lord,

Thank You for teaching me that You always hear my prayers. Help me to know You more and more by teaching me more about You. In Jesus's name. Amen.

# GLOSSARY

Astrologers—Those who attempt to predict the future through distant stars and other heavenly bodies.

Daniel—Jewish noble from Israel's royal household. Daniel was one of the Jewish captives exiled to Babylon and chosen to be trained in Babylonian ways.

King Nebuchadnezzar II (neh-buh-kuhd-neh-zr)—Babylonian king who ruled between August 605 BC and October 562 BC

Magicians—Scribes who were acquainted with the occult arts.

Sorcerers—Those who mixed ingredients for magical purposes.

Printed in the United States
by Baker & Taylor Publisher Services